A Seek and Find
Adventure in the Desert

The Adventures of Hum

Bonnie Miller

ISBN 978-1-64349-985-7 (paperback)
ISBN 978-1-64515-833-2 (hardcover)
ISBN 978-1-64349-986-4 (digital)

Christian Faith Publishing, Inc.
832 Park Avenue
Meadville, PA 16335
www.christianfaithpublishing.com

Printed in the United States of America

God created all things. The animals do not worry about how to get their food. God created ways for animals to adapt to their habitats so they can survive on the earth. Here is a story about a bird seeking to find his best friend to share the great news that God is so good, as you learn about adaptations: pollination, mimicry, mutualism, and camouflage.

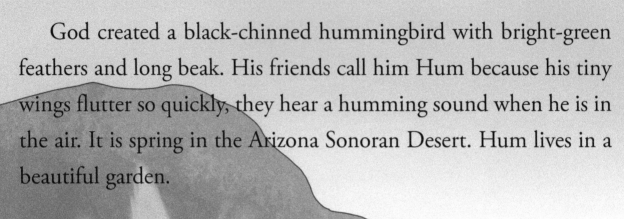

God created a black-chinned hummingbird with bright-green feathers and long beak. His friends call him Hum because his tiny wings flutter so quickly, they hear a humming sound when he is in the air. It is spring in the Arizona Sonoran Desert. Hum lives in a beautiful garden.

Hum is hungry, so he stops by the ocotillo plant to drink the nectar from the orange flowers. As he enjoys the sweet, tasty treat, he thinks, *God is so good to provide such a tasty meal! I do not worry about what I will eat because God watches over all the creatures of the desert. He even gave me my best friend, desert tortoise. Now where is he?*

Can you help him find his friend, the desert tortoise?

Hum decides to go ask the butterfly if he has seen Tortoise. Hum knew the viceroy butterfly. Vic was his friend, so he shouted up to the saguaro cactus blossom where Vic was rubbing pollen all over his body, asking sweetly, "Have you seen my friend, the desert tortoise?"

Vic looked down and around the landscape but could not see the tortoise. He said, "No, I am sorry, but I do not see Tortoise."

Do you see the desert tortoise?

Now monarch butterfly was lurking nearby in a creosote bush. God made these butterflies nearly alike for protection. Hum's mother had told him to be aware of these two butterflies because the monarch was poisonous to many insects and birds! The viceroy butterfly has a black line across his hind wing. He is not poisonous.

Do you see the difference? One mimics the other. This is called mimicry.

Hum decides to go ask the brown bat if he has seen his friend, the desert tortoise. Brown bat loves to drink the nectar from the cholla cactus blossoms and spreads the pollen for the cactus, too. This is part of pollination. The flower on this cactus only blooms at night! This is perfect for the bat, who is awake at night. God arranged a mutual agreement for them to help each other survive. This is called mutualism.

Bat had not seen Tortoise either because he was sleeping while hanging upside down on a branch of a mesquite tree. Hum decides not to wake his friend, the brown bat. As he was leaving, Hum thought about how good God is to give them so much!

Do you see Tortoise?

Hum is getting worried about his friend! He has not seen him all day! He decides to go ask the gray coyote for help. He searches but cannot find coyote. He began to chirp loudly for coyote. God made coyote the same color as his surroundings for protection. This is called camouflage.

Do you see the coyote?

Suddenly, he jumps out from near a rock and says, "Hello, Hum. I have been napping after my delicious lunch. Why are you chirping so loudly? Are you in trouble again?"

They laugh together as Hum explains his search. "God is so good to us to give us good friends."

Coyote had not spotted Tortoise either. Do you see Tortoise?

Hum flew all around the garden searching for his friend. He was getting tired! He decides he should go back to the entrance of the garden to try to find Tortoise one more time because it is getting late in the afternoon.

As he was entering the dirt path, he realized that Tortoise was in a small hole by the butterfly bush. He was just waking up from a nice long nap. He had found Tortoise!

When Hum saw Tortoise, he was so happy to have found his friend! He sang loudly, "God is so good! He helped me find you, my friend!"

Tortoise looked up and smiled at Hum because he felt blessed to have such a good friend!

About the Author

Bonnie Miller is a retired educator. She loves the Lord and is thankful for His blessings. She enjoys spending time with her family and reading to her granddaughter. She dedicates this book to her best friend, Gwynda, who always told her she should write a children's book about science. The Sonoran Desert is a beautiful place to live, so she hopes you enjoy learning about its many wonders!

CPSIA information can be obtained
at www.ICGtesting.com
Printed in the USA
BVHW022358041119
562845BV00033B/293/P

9 781645 158332